Dichten=
No. 9

Ulf Stolterfoht

LINGOS I-IX

translated from the German
by Rosmarie Waldrop

Burning Deck/Anyart, Providence

DICHTEN = is a (not quite) annual of current German language writing in English translation. Most issues are given to the work of a single author.
Editor: Rosmarie Waldrop.

Individual copies: $14
Subscription for 2 issues: $23 postpaid

Distributors:
Small Press Distribution, 1341 Seventh St., Berkeley, CA 94710
1-800/869-7553; www.spdbooks.org
Spectacular Diseases, c/o Paul Green, 83b London Rd., Peterborough, Cambs. PE2 9BS
H-Press, www.hpress.no

for US subscriptions only:
Burning Deck, 71 Elmgrove Ave., Providence RI 02906

Parts of the translation were first published in *Aufgabe, Circumference, NO: a Journal of the Arts, The Canary, Two Lines,* and the online journals *Coconut* and *Fascicle.*
Section VI was published as a chapbook, *Lingos,* by Cuneiform Press in Buffalo, NY.

Burning Deck is the literature program of Anyart: Contemporary Arts Center, a tax-exempt (501c3), non-profit corporation.

ISSN 1077-4203
ISBN 978-1-886224-85-8

Contents

LINGOS IV

LINGOS V

LINGOS VI: mothertongues

LINGOS VII

LINGOS VIII

LINGOS IX

LINGOS I

(1)

he also verb meanly enough into the noun
breeds his good cause so stantive under pre
as he says / if he throws — now punctuates
the inter or tactically presses it with with

in part how far — a leading question —
craving and gender are willing to share
a role in whose: ramified case of big bang
aftermath in zwolle or half-mast colon

infusion in walk-tide — he verb it just right:
inflects the flecked beast but injects no
future around ur-conjunct or aur-adject
he'll infinite and deeper yet for

clature lies heavy on his nomen: when to
close the *if*-clause out of the frying pan from
rela on — if sub ordinates the tone? over
pluperfect metals let thickets grow thick

(2)

whosever coat-tail after coat-tail your
endeavor to compose now so thicktitiously
engenders what fuel-fucking self-destructive
higgledy-piggery you so seriously unbody

or hardly blessed among root veggies
when ham's smoked in the half-left field
you cross your heart over hide's enticement
and all that cohabits genetically unknot

which you in heat and under oath endorse
knowing the ombudsman's enleathering a
breedin' shame like pidgin in gdingen as your
be-true-to-me you so endearingly unmarry

where for your club-moss name you will be
envied hallowed be thy come forfeit engorged
covetous deeply how you and gdansk
instinct and body tissue unself and unsex

(3)

aforesaid man in childbed whose wing-beat
had flagged lazily this side of however
veined a feeling/pained a hazing then
cleared "xanten" his throat or rather reared

preverbs of far and wide nobody hides the
chaff from the wheat from the fries likewise
he has no grasp on copula or copulation
while reek of leaks he also seeks not to forget

to name whose cheeky cherishing of so ex-
clusive an inclusion via the need to cover
debts brought into marriage beside missing
each other in the extreme took hounds to

pfronten with lowest unction/higher mash to
multi-avoid the enmeshed (ablutions/offerings/
unleavened skin) no shortage ever of evermore
schisms but maybe of guts to go for the edge...

(4)

the moscovite bends sailor ears she
wants his chin he says because her
own got smashed anno the capture
of kronstadt (kuhlmann had already

in lübeck been fitted out with a blue-
and-white suit we know he never
took off) but all so dense so sluggish
so crude back then in leiden where

(how well the other man was dressed)
a fear
ful hemorrhage pointed spring-
impulse "to breslau:" very very hot
via livonia to stambul (hast not been

published?) on to strassbourg and
their now inevitable rapprochement
— blow-stunned one so he burned on
— ablaze the sailor so he lay slain

(5)

at first hardly more blighted than indo-
causal not unlike a walking stick off on
a run as it were toward — let's just say
canoer's luck. in the backyards of tampere

they cast a cold eye as he capsized though
didn't look down their noses in this
respectacle. was said to hire out as a jazz
musician and draw crowds at bashes in the

franzensfeste to have tried experiments like:
caulked his canoe's inside with franken bread
and resin (black and greasy who so much
as touches it) and so on. barely worth while

the rest and quickly told: more and more
forgets to dish up wash down and gets lost
among the iroquois only to once more —
which so far he hesitates to presume known

(6)

no way out i must turn farmhand
have pitchfork stihl-saw telemarrow
and am supposed toward dawn amid
snow flurries to fend off with stun-

gun (electric) the pack of black oh
boars heading here from calw and
as every morning put up the beet-
feed stack the cord of wood when

the carinthian guys showed up in
a vw "passat" and brought more
saws and crowbars never changed
their shirts only the stihl-saw chain

and then drove off again and paul
held forth it was just possible he'd
known a certain herr cules and
threw into the fire his rubber boots

(7)

if necessary "spastic-tongued" as
if not having got the goat you —
what: pull off its hide? new para-
graph transition to a) the city that

my grandfather maintains is inns-
bruck b) the hedgehogs we call
truffels c) the memory of vaguely
"carving your bear before he escapes."

further: we'll telephone each touch
or keep in other. it's not beyond the
pale but on a cowhide we'll be found:
if need be sticking out our tongues.

and "and" only suggested here.
and a feeling that a pelt is fearsome
yet also close-to-the-gut only for him
who's starved to make his world.

got up into the nties. their fits. by defiance or force
born: foaming. absences among the shrubs. they
form a milieu. they convulse saliva-coagulation
pills. though barely into the red-scale like shrill.

were circa paprika on the ring. there recognized a
guy making a buchholz speech distinctive scent
around the neck. breeder's insignia. mediately
orders pils for two. then back home to convulse. at

least however: ratty civvies leather hat and beard
direction *"exeo in a spasm."* right in the city. they fell
in fits without attracting notice. hair parted side-
ways garners women's praise. tuft on top. but not

spectacular. it was an in-between for both. they
represent relationship. within the framework of
their throes OK. tied willy-nilly: they resent copu-
lation. present themselves and without shame.

(9)

hybrid stole the show he falsettoed (a jack of
all food a sassa of fras) pigging out refluxes
acid. horror: his *stomach*. to you he whimpers:
boy ass/mustard gas/vienna in the teens where

places he disliked were counted studios — that
guy! a passionate toad (*besame mucho*) twirls
girls of both classes: shivers as never before
the drapery. was monkey hair. was house-

holder with green/flutey voice: some sweets
my dear? high and mighty for our lady of the
komsomol (second taint: quit in 'nineteen) and
ever since refreshingly fat a king of the waltz:

"halt" almost as if we heard him — right? while
klux infanta strolls along the bank springtimes
of blondness already piled high. thus he comes
on: the frog nature of green eyes. her waterbed.

LINGOS II

Looking languidly at a pair of tin snips,
and then deciding to call them tin snips
— what a burst of glory!

—donald barthelme

(1)

talent in rut the artier foreign pseudo-
prop gali or matias like cognates like
consorts not honey to dialect ears: they
mangle phonemes chaste and german

pondering this and yet in spite of and /
or signs of break-down WANT IT: shall
then for agit's sake the anti (i.e. now)
though quasi's barely born flounder

in meaning-mania scarcely veiled as
long as glyph stands among runes? the
author's last osmosis unmuzzles hiero /
ditto pidgin manuscripts: so torted dis

like ball's "goramen" as well as latent
INDO-WANT: go roll yourself a syllable
play horse to foreign carts to *intro-
ducing* mix-o-lydian (where disparate

particles demonstrate non-success:
the innermost mongolia / the uttermost-
ly prickly beard) the hermeneuts of *art*
however construe IT as rather diffident

and dank what actually (what actually
"exists but at the moment of its
simulation") should after all be called
methinks — and so still pondering all this...

(2)

abruptly herder appeared together with job
to diaper the oceans as babies one does.
speaking as from the times of sirach that
some remains of essence forced the hybrid

toward hameln like a ram in a storm.
("arsenals of snow and hail/sky water-
ways — who would like that?") confuses
you of course: where's the salvation! that's

why about a hundred years of bauhaus
were leaning at the bar to cuss it dis. of
which we got to hear a rare: discourse
gone long in the extreme. so even they!

dream of the orient. sings and answers
questions. was there war in the street?
flamingoes in fruitfight always futuristic-
perfect. thereafter years on the job stooped —

"crossing gate"— on the rail embankment:
he on the contrary noticed lack of such.
here was the point to end stillborn creation
so-called. says herder and describes it

further: who could and would compose
like these? says herder maybe after all: i
hardly can imagine such a thing. yet crimi-
nal the attempt at same is nevertheless not.

(3)

i feel as in a zipper's teeth: to die. and
in quotation to be burning vie. and say.
but he maintains to: the bitter end. we'll
just go live in pomerania. we'll just go

light the pumpkin. urns to us upon my
word autistic. however nightly the owl's
flight the threat is scarcely less for it.
quite on the contrary. taught goethe

years ago that if the fox is dead what
matters is his hide. and that the thumb
is means to grasp not just part of the
hand. and "please in your bond of wound"

let not him buried be in his skin. for
first let this be to his credit: to omit the
rarara of bonding as also stated by third
parties: for once we're saddled in for it.

viz. secondly. so. arises the question if it
helps to nail the badger his pelt on the
wall. of his burrow the hunters by the way
not. rather the urgent wish to have it all

promptly settled. so. i feel as palliative:
my appointment. for life on foot. high-
strung bow-string. or more sassily: it all
fits in one jar. seen from sufficiently afar.

(4)

that it's precisely not OK: not to
see the murky. when it's right there.
means milk maybe but suddenly
brings up opaque. this by hear-say

at the time westphalia (bochum). still
hardly like much else alas alas. the
point of fact remained a dirty river
(emscher). and what I took for such.

a beer-jaunt. burned-out torches above
the ruhr. always thirsty in the dark. alone
in the cellar the finisters. (they alone
luminous. kept hidden from the eye.)

that sweet is murkiness to human
sight. a sign of grace. and yes in this
way much like beer: today shalt be
with me in paradise. thou art my *kindl.*

to shelter the murk from greedy eyes.
cellar. certain infringements taking place.
"and yet were once..." and not divorced
as long as content promised cover.

but look: all inner effervescence gone!
unhandsome dead that's what we'll
be. naturally conceivable to wallow
in the murk. natural conceivably.

(5)

proposition: only what's pickled in like
brine will be as nine-eyes is to blind
(i.e. as if the eucharist) — test: palate
on dried cod for who has eyes to see

as an example how maybe "ass" was said
in gettysburg and meant the landlord /
even as a child he knew 'twas rats
they ate on board and he'd not be the

first to eat the salt to lick the antlers
certainly scratch udders for the milk-
idea: a whirring wire pulled through
low-fat cheese idea of being conscripted

to: yes hunger when stockpails run dry
and burst with vinegar and just as now
it seems back then everything got
rated by how suited for the stockpot

(verdict — the skinnier ones might
remember — almost always positive)
notice too the gnashing of teeth in the
process: he sucked on rotting wetness

(the most tender-hearted may well empa-
thize: the first mate's belly was the last
to disappear cost-lost on the upper edge
of the frame.) proposition: for he had.

(6)

all ears especially as they of course
never came from outside but still were
definitely heard as can be checked: "we
here need to appease a yellow" he hears

and later they say does it. for heaven's
sake then to encourage (with image-
blind compulsion) a bright red you may
in matters of black on white be sure of

inspiration: he'll lure the gray OK. to
listen to obey the urge (in words:
wait for commands to surge) to loop
the rope around the lantern and be

granted to unmope. does he already
feel the fine thread's tender tie/the
strong rope's goodly shade from one
ear to it will be asked: the other?

all neck in these affinities elective
hardly. triple to ever more gordian the
knot of almost theft of a crust of bread
and never touch. in plain speech: properly

secular equals "can be got by ruse."
poaching in foreign fields incriminated
as NULL-ART/the diagnosis hurts:
case of attempted infiltration-fraud.

(7)

knowing such disdoings whimpering "turbance"
that in malchow where although in bed we
dreamed: of sitting on a chair. so that (some
people's dreams are grand!) "inwardly

stirred but outwardly tied like gulliver"
(yet to be proven: turbance means storm
of stimuli) some rain came down WHICH
— mecklenburger mercy shower/we

guess the point — WAS VERY DRY. and yet
fell under rain. and in reverse the reverse
is just as likely: thought of chair beats
condition of bed. and sleeping under such.

knowing of clenched "muscles did not
make an undue bulge in the suit" so that
strangely — coming from güstrow now—
we felt: we were inside one skin/we

threatened: to succumb to influence. how
it all then slipped away. (intrudes the
memory of the tin snip. remains to say of
what.) glass-hard presentiment takes root:

every thing must bear a name. its appelation.
therefore muscles chair and bed. if we how-
ever is uncertain. last period punched in
tin. something to chew on for some time.

(8)

beautiful like: latent snap decayward —
because abstract. horrible like the death
screams of hedgehogs as they fade into
the night. that's what the new poetry

is like. there was a time when man
rather at one with fear grew pale in
all the colors of the garden. and birds
with grief dropped from the trees.

dreadful like: headlong into cod —
because concrete. ("do you consider
my methods morbid?" "sir, i can't discern
no method anywhere!") refrain:

beautiful's not the beautiful phrase.
beautiful's not the beauti... ad libitum.
beautiful is the chopping of chickens.
but not religion for all that. whereas:

"made to beat like a fake heart in a real
animal's real body" — because this
sounds german. the cleaning of fish. the
reaping of robins. the sagging of hose

(says r.) — concrete it's not but possible
if only because the song moves us
to tears? beautiful is only the abstract.
because construct. now all together:

(refrain)

(9)

came a man talked improbability and state of.
organized himself and the matter to nearly
ninety out of a hundred. which was high
considering how fragile these "constructions

of wire wood and linen IN WHICH THEY FLEW
WITHOUT A PARACHUTE." almost coarse in
comparison says böhme the vessels of the
spirit that mirror the essence of things.

said adam before the fall were laughing mad-
ly and flying through our teeth the blue off
the sky — as against — "'the few who under-
stood something' — of what?" is about how

it will end. (in search of the uncouth word:
alfa. bravo. charlie. delta. echo. echo: they
so would have liked to see the zoo of oulu.
more obscure: let form unmorph i into u —

sometimes it works sometimes it doesn't.)
came a man talked improbability and state
of. carried the germ of it already at this
time. veins aflow with bromine. so he

engendered without offspring. taking
possible for proven. came spoke and stood:
WASPWAISTED WASPLIGHT STILL TRIM
VICIOUS SMALL AND IMMOBILE. contaminated.

LINGOS III

re-encounter with *cut-mute*

albeit/much less
summer'd leave unsaid

what otherwise is told by steel. even as-
suming ARE DUBBED it were these stanzas
cold and smooth that here unfold to full
sensation — is this still klopstock or already:
whereof language can but stammer? but
this is me who seem to glimmer like a box

tree. in the margins mutterings are heard
that by this rule you might as well FORBID
YOUNG METAL TO SHIMMER! exactly this
they did and so. breaks off. whereupon of
course applause: the honey / not the flutter
of wings. breaks off. breaks off. the man

who witnessed christian tears — this is by
no means me — close to whose heart the
flutter of wings. who nevertheless has a taste
for honey. a little time goes by. breaks off
soon after probably. wherein no splendor
buried lies unless 'twere to erect ("larger

montage-like structures where chaos
more than shimmers through" — see also
METAL!) but instead: breaks off. later
there was talk of things shooting up in
sheaves. of uncouth youth and of the
prater. the rest much less be left unsaid.

now he reads his fill in flesh/
(translate)/wrecks all torn/
a sentencestorm

of the type "easily as recognized that"
blindly stands in literally this context.
most arbitrary. he declares. hears HEARS
not to say crypticly cryph murmurings
"excessively banked" that language is a
weapon and sounds to him almost like kill.

analogous in kind i.e. amalgamized. as in
please ferryman translate what by your leave
so crudely prospers: that *nichtungsdichtung's*
possible — the same old hat: out of deepest
amazement anger/never appeasing. up to here
modest rather than dripping with tolerance: *now*

he gives the lie the harmful class will "later be
permitted to reply:" TENDER kills right away.
TOUGH more by detours. hours later conjures
CRITTERS. concurs BEGUILED: that inner
voices start to flimmer: first this. then that.
then those. then THAN cracks in this kind

of wood: rather generically "pleasant spot." per-
haps: eskimo women that sing into each other's
mouth — yes they exist. kills by no means.
perhaps: cold feet when faced with one's own
text. twitters-in-the-twigs an epidemic. enter
the not-identical. "the knave of pain steals off."

do knives do knives/
truly dismember/
do they cut wool after wool

as we too lunge through barriers between
hermetic and silesic by weaving in this
grave suspicion: here versions of detention
are taking place. we have documents that
(1) not only was polish spoken in secret but
(2) a good part of the population THOUGHT

in polish. cut. *drops steady upper underarms/*
water standing or vessels seems *reminiscent*
of veins/the words in their distress juggle a
red mess. for instance also this: the tossing
of the finger of his very own father —
has composition. has truth function.

the fiery young by non-virtue-criteria like guts
and ever ready — have dash. have pluck's
nimble unruly patchwork. we however
have documents of super-meta-quality:
that (3) the war year '42 saw prosecution of:
speech offenders. for gross misdemeanor.

hello maximum sentence. hello hearing the
layers underneath (correct) but believe with
an extra ache: focus on depth we need. old
solingen plunges in. as we too lunge through
limitations: *steady drops/*mutual taps. cut.
then graft both together for form's sake.

as per in memory/of word-stumps/
watch by all means/how they hook and

crook: they now had. long enough in foreign
service been. should they begin to grow or
shrink they still would. rather less inflect than
loot the dialect. rumors distort. users report:
are willing. to mutiny a stand against. their
shrill in good stead SYNTAX-scream. succumbs

to NEGLECT. (...*purged of the urge* and then *goes
numb*). they say: "the word that's tied to might
will wither." this means also: when not subject
to any master — name the master. means roughly
to distinguish: *sheer* and *mere*. *scarce* and *cash*.
fallow will step in when athwart drops out.

athwart makes superclear: sometimes foreign-
ness sets free. private perty propulses indenture
at home. only the incomprehensible belongs.
especially to users. (those were the days: one
didn't know how subversive it is to make eyes
at "belong." but knew instinctively: dear mother-

tongue — burned down! and therefore rarely
used her nouns. still frowned at nowadays how-
ever the other taboo: "that i as if in madness
now / in crazy songs must speak"). NEGLECT-call
of the second kind: CONTRA PURGE / PRO URGE.
this precisely "is what so distresseth me."

twice-told tale/fox-in-flight/
mortar-and-pestle/noggin-and-goose

st. augustine already knew this when he
said: oh-these-gallows-again / ah-how-
they-thrive — that sentences are just long
names. i-however-quote: could not find
such a passage in st. augustine. latch on (an
irishman sharply advised) to thrice-told

tales "how green was my valley / how very
puritan my f-word" while the other whispers:
know-nothing / act-as-if / act-as-if. I will adaft.
yes yes: i'll breed myself thorough. end up
breaking my little neck (in mission "borussia")
and declare: i wish to be alimbed in pairs.

thus accelerated speed is to distance as fabled
sentence is to word. as word to name. so it's the
poet's task to clarify: can "needy means *bedürftig*"
be further analyzed? if yes: does pumpkin /
pumped-to-the-chin speak through me / for itself
or even "testify?" this kind of question. the same

man must have had in mind when suddenly he
quotes and hollers: "what, you skunk don't want
to talk rot? ah go ahead and talk rot, it don't
mean shit!" i-however-could-not-find-a-soul who
kneads his words as if they contained names.
(what — if they too were only husks — then?)

you'd hear the heat/hot equals loud
an open pulse/such gaping
handiwork/such perfect red

if/then: in all due form — baroque code
threatens to mob: cried defied and loosely
tied — we need a treatise on knots: synes-
thesia. palm fronds. theory of refrigeration.
done: one can see one's hand in front of one's
eyes! and with a kiss i hand on my artsycraft.

soon/when: after years of emotion — the
rift's at most still dimly felt. young shaman's
silence short is cut: to be touched he's evi-
dently not. un-tamer in his element: even
to splice a denser message. is idolatry.
is devilry. requires stricter pandering.

if/though: this knowledge is a secret/blabbed
it quickly loses strength — but to reveal the
structure is allowed? from IS to infer sense
— is? he brokers with a bite: it is! at no loss
for examples: "childbirth IS thirsty work."
chicken hearts ARE exciting fare. likewise

WOULD BE good: relation of young goiter to
saddle nose. and — as every bullet knows
"tin never IS narrow and thick." finished.
almost without loss of hardness. one can
reconstruct the pattern. on i hand it out of
need. by virtue of most willing. i remain.

fraught with naught

the unbridled increase of tongues the
constant rattling of words in the morning
the evening the unceasing pulse of things
to think of even in sleep the eternal ham-
mering of phrases like "in sight of night"
by and by begin to fill mouth after mouth.

the swarming-around-me of birds. in
order to make (to name) your escape you
undertake the reconstruction of lungs to
bellows / deconstruction of feather to quill
(must be a flight log) and tiniest fictions
germinate inward. featherbed fictions.

like ideas functions of THE I: that i were
words. and words therefore were me. THE
I can't grasp it. it as it were grasps me.
thus we seem to form a team: THE I hates
birds. birds are like me: feathered but
untarred. like flews entirely unlicked.

by feathers bird tongues voices. they:
understand a good day's work as the
destruction of what came before. i: con-
sider there might be facts outside the
poem. they: "a handsome *hulk*." i: a
brutish wimp. amid. but actually replaced.

how without as if to namely/
will have to be affirmed in silence

my hanging down from me on my right
and left pieces of flesh repeated each in
fivefold branchings that seem similar or
same even farther down: tubes to be
verified by touch (they seem indeed to be
mine). such attention must lead to compre-

hension. steals over me alarm as arm reaches
round to: itself: an arm. 'twould melt a bone
to understand: here overlap two states.
hunter is deer and deer hunter. as if we said:
stone. and blue and small and cool and
round and knew: sweet. and tasted sour.

but for this we'd have no word. sated / still.
would break the finicky fine-tuned structure
as squirrel cracks the winter's nuts: without
as if. or as (as similate) or buts. this would be
bitter, true — a word we use if things do get
too bitter: and use with "as" as people do.

"as if amputated" as sheer pleasure when
certain parts (say arms or legs my own)
are being cut off or dropping all alone. they
need be there in pairs. my each-case-feeling
of own as foreign with alas as-if-distortion's
such that no-one can with certainty say: thus.

fistsize words/wounds

(eg the wound BECAUSE) for if we picture the
thinker then altogether bold. does frege perhaps
fretfully ask "horse?" as a matter of course he
does not. to him a concept is a thing. meaning
even passion. as for an outside world no doubt
is gnawing at him. and yet: of unavoidable we

have to speak. of hard language when he
claims: the city of berlin's a city. volcano
vesuvius a volcano. the wound BECAUSE might
well be ditto. according to him it is not.
to him falsehood is true value. a song of
songs. and art how lithe his language sounds.

far out begins a rumbling. of meta-stuff/
cognition-increase/sense. begins with: "i was there.
i have experienced the BECAUSE." shows wounds.
and leaves. such terse confession is remembered
long. has unheard-of effect. however: calling his
"experience BECAUSE" — this far we haven't got.

let us picture the thinker then: as a young beast.
speckled. bashful. nicely with scruples hung.
gutshot and pup-shy he is in generating the
BECAUSE. let us picture the thinker: frail he
leans against the snow and wind. and then:
we really see the thinker in front of our eyes.

LINGOS IV

(1)

opens brightly: sentences exist. closes claims:
they're filled with words. and that is all there's
to it. in overtones a merely as what's surely
common: goodly perception of fruit — may well
stand in for other things. complete perception
of goodly fruit — here's how it functions:

like apples eyes and. not to mention pears. presumes
pending corroboration: the apple does not see itself.
in this it's like the eye. you can't tell from the looks
of one (please look on this as a sentence) that it is
looked at by another. "please look on this as a
sentence" likewise to be looked on as a sentence etc.

"is to say" takes place. aspects apace. one owes /
thanks / is obliged. "is to mean" obstructs. "more
later" belongs here. strong feeling of happiness
through fruit. a newer. a better. a dapper perhaps.
perhaps mere structures but at least crude and
pure. leads from needy to approximate. the word

of fruit in the beholder's eye. the post as beam
or mote. the sentence of the hereditary branch.
the word trunk ambiguous. now: wrong
fruit in the right place. then: the tree as word —
a goodly sentence. then if i'm not mistaken
the whole tree on the left as strongest branch.

what still remains of "songless" — "an earnest
bird" brings up. no earnest bird debates what
seemed essentially the fact. he cancels as it were
himself. you mentally shake your head. you nod.
you see. this must the essence of negation be.
what is confusing at a second glance:... NO X

HORSES (... carry you away) at third glance will
hold up and fast. no one horse holds so fast.
nine horses or eleven: carry you away. exactly
as no ten. they hold you fast. then let's have at
no zero horses — to sidle/bridle up! a matter

(to remove last lingering doubts): not not
to be neglected. not to forget: forget. to be
hungry. simply done. resolved: to cut the
bread. forgets. must now (the bread gets
harder and harder) to cut be called to "saw"?
may your speech at best be yea yea/nay nay!

what's likewise hard to clarify: if perhaps probably
exists. tendency: perhaps. probably not. but here
you quickly stand alone. and can't help make a
stand for granting "nonsense absolute" to have to
sense make some. unprofitable enterprise: not only
not to say not/but to do un. and then its beauty too.

(3)

while as late as 1874 it was supposed
that green was a simple color we later
proceeded to. starting from this point could
be anticipated possibilities two: either/or.
either "heaven knows what the colorblind
really see" (schulte) or: heaven does not.

where referred explicitly to green. so WHILE
stayed unexamined though it was there (as in
the heilbronn slaughter-house) that "all strands
came together:" partly with/partly without.
partly in any case with: a multiplicity in part spell-
bound. would designate one strand. and does.

strand 1) everything goes according to plan: even
while we utter e.g. "quail damage"/establish
the danger of — much pushes in directions like:
mere ditty or heredity? much seems to point
to that (strand 2) this time the possibilities
are three: defective percept. defective con-

cept. — says schulte: or both! we by the way
incline decidedly toward ditty. decisive this (see
also above) is not. it was a hard road from yellow
to blue. we had to be rigged out. there were
vibrations as of red in green. we had to settle in.
we've come to circa '50: and meanwhile to terms.

(4)

critico/traditional: why does scream inaudibly
rather than suddenly fall silent while at least
according to the ear in-difference was the given
we described manico/syntactically "the secret of
one=self in terms of interior decoration:" table
lamp chair & bed lamented on the other hand and

in a voice of deep jaw-potent purple consternation
increasing "vechtation" of the spirit (literary) (and
our part in it) instead of: let's go friends! where
meaning's born replying to gaelic "forka need?"
with hearty TAUF TAUF only to be saddle-braised
and then gasp our last. clinico/experimental:

"the softness compressed within its uniform of
hitler-flesh" that literally strikes you dead. the
way things fall apart: the lily ravished. worm
lavished. song suddenly silenced. razes me to
fertile ground. raises instinct into botany. as the
wind blows/so the vote goes: insane construct

to outlaw sensuality once and for all. critico/
traditional: if images at all let them be bad.
manico/syntactical: image mock-ups. bogus attacks.
clinico/experimental: "talis is a word abused
in many passims. I am developing right now a
quantum theory of this" — mangy-o/frontal.

(5)

morphed orphic. nonword sils. for want of
tongue an ersatz-orplid. doubly docile toward
a quasi stopgap october. the unstrut river's
deficit in oxygen. vaihinger's merry ascent
to copdom. wood smoke. november. smell
sediment where late sweet buntings sang.

shoots now its tributary toward promised
dead-arm delta. topic erased. twelve inches
of the best left open. waiblinger's descent into
the cave. smelting to fill the purse. sweet
howitzers across the land. forced feel in sepia
swallowtailed: to muddle the elm. to coddle

the cause. to suckle for two. morsed ugric.
to make writing shy of thinking. flurries
december. profanest kraken winter. ultima
thule — predated. gleim's admission to the
club. by the way "soberly put: for sheer
pleasure / uplift — even his best will hardly."

so much for "syllableless communication."
gluck's late farewell to his audience. horse-
pitality. districted pigpen. this might after all
be the end. unwhorfed form. scattered chirps.
not loud but with the customary brittle.
accordingly incorporated in the corpus.

(6)

unexpectedly doesn't arrive — quite retro rather
what comes rolling in as text: half musty half de-
caying breath (discard after 02) a hundred years
of mushrooms to wade through/bizarre centenary.
rhizome scenarios so far seem to charm the art-
brat. till crisis of expression "makes him quake."

sensing the sense-cadaver's nameless shattering
as its last chance a lyric i enters the dance with
breeze-precision counter-wheeze and honey-
sweet soliciting: "come here what ables has to syll
— come here! I still take good care of my sentences.
am shepherd and lord to the poor old word/of

scattered phonemes the safe port." materials
took this in surprised. mildly, it must be said.
result "accordingly" called STOP THE POETIC
MOM-AND-POPS and slaughterhouses respective-
ly (destruction's got to be a twin!): the terrors
of a fox farm while the beasts are skinned.

the exuberance in the butcher's stance: what could
come has and pleases/"falls to pieces" as well as —
we're talking concepts: pellet drop/system prop.
what now still laps turns into non-committal slop.
the wound's lip bulges into stump. in pop speech
protein grows rank. and litterature upheaves its cart.

(7)

now that it profiteth the literary front to mangle
(NOT that i want BACK BEHIND to crafty crumbling)
the ground of neo-chopup's rigging is undone
"for the soldier in hot straits" whose pain falls
silent in its pain — does there remain a word to
say how one is crushed? its gnawing quality clots

"was blind" and sore spot in the mouth report: he
not just speaks/he also acts that way — gets blurred.
so crush scrapes a) just barely by where b) the rows
of teeth snap shut. on inklings of forced labor: they
would dig up far bigger things! there follows audible
grind of "chewed away." the mouth lets go the rest.

"...monsters premature births fruit aborted before
growth rain in the wastelands..." etc. — kinds of
creatures between bark and tree. gently we must
lift them from the battlefield. whereupon reunion
of the maimed prepares the writing desk to win
the war. and lo the butchery seems compelling.

not back behind what's on the page (because the
loveliness of mutilation) even crushing threatens
to succeed. the sense of din in every thing: "once
i too was in this *kim*" is grim. for want of words
to say how we lament (especially when pain
degrades to misery): take this as our last gift.

(in memory ernst herbeck)

(8)

"borrowed lynx eyes from common rhyme-
and-reason-sense" to decode rests of
palimpsests in shorthand remap concept-
scraps with badger paws scratch off scrape
down the recent layers "to compare the
more keen-sightedly the qualities of things."

corpse in(tro)spection. from words that grow
tangible "once they mightily neighborly groan"
via a lyrico-typical sound-strut "hybrid"
straight to pseudo-vico's "place before time"
— overwhelming fragments. but something
still resists. there is a threat of other tones.

attempts in mutant meter. manipulated
metronome. compulsive forte-bark at passages
marked. especially in complex sentences
make form conscious of itself. and that's just
the beginning. the current state of sound:
good. the tone *gestalt* however lags behind.

skirmishes with sense continue. the dogged
look of the compound sentence. it is the last to
pass with thanks. thus you disband a position.
a foreign scalp most decorative. thus you unmask
a pose. the barbarism of abstraction. poetry
hurrah! language is allowed to obey vision.

(9)

your most obedient doing duty to critique
your honor's art-weave's non-bombast pre-
sume to prove to make it known a paragon:
takes care to prune anew. these lines are
running on. how easily your talent is turned
to account seems crystal-clearly characteristic

of a scout. but too bright light remains in
doubt. although a place of great sophistication
with downright sponger qualities. as if a part
of further most diligent attempts to help as
usual ourselves. so that we finally put on
some text. but then, say, jena. thuringian con-

ditions. the back-in-anger look is missing.
there really have been goings-on: those
slippery dogs this walk on water and alas
rearmament. spoken through gaps. never
more broken. flexed pallaksch-athena-
fragments of the lords of indisputable.

life maintained in language-heft. whose "in-
herent" nevertheless afflicted with. the pus
"inherent" in these easter bells — just have
a look! look how the dear old willows sway.
i would like best to rustle rushes. how easily
languages come off the bone — just have a look.

LINGOS V

"eyegrowing wind, blowing eyes — this kind of thing just doesn't exist!"

—peter gosse

(1)

distinctions are good or the attempt at a
fight with letters "lick my pelt but don't
get me wet" when on the 9th of march 1940

old man in runic rapture laid down his arms
(...but every time he scored was PICKLED PINK
AS A KING — konradin and so on) in the year

of kleist "aspired to klopstockian greatness"
who succeeded in parting the fur from the
beast. (attempted with a real fox! proof of

leakage currents in the top layer of hair / wire-
haired!) only to terminally senesce. by the
same right the furrier here maketh his mark.

we however confuse our dates:
pre-march is after all bright logic. as
was. will be. is is often the desire

"to explain the pictures to the dead hare."
in conflict grows what separates: we can-
not skin AND trader be. said languages

draw on or the attempt at sub-
stitute acts "lend me a word but
burst the form" or leave me alone.

(2)

**and was perceptible the growth and the
syrian soil shattered and flamelike under-
foot stinging and nausea over me comes**

from raving hunger so that although the
phrase contains no BURNS the innermost
from the outer turns: it's in the gut begins

the orient! but what's for world and body
meant (that both here coincide) mutates per
image to its opposite: only who "branchless"

calls the rain can know how loud the ivy hangs.
who listens now to goodly words (like glandular
twang and self-intoxication) will see his ear in

lynxlike manner bloom. damascus however
(plundered! and featherweight at catching voices):
is the navel of this earth — a hardly hoped-for

babel. from hunger namely as noise. from the
dark trade of stomach of liver. from the finicky
work of the kidneys — severed by into and nation.

remains to discuss. always preposterous:
the riot run by weeds. perceptibly a tree breaks
into leaf. the woods pick up and follow orpheus.

(3)

**but let not our fatherland become for
us too small a space. hard to lie on
with our feet and hands too. just air.**

for flight. for lies the flow-speed of
light. the lens's drift. the soil deceived.
let it be cramped! the crumb that never

saw a plow. the peasant woman's iodine
deficiency. how fast the water runs in
straits. in stride a light sting in the crotch.

the milk spilt. laughing allowed. it
must be fuckin possible to change
the district from a to b.

is short what wide seems like a line?
how broad is long allowed to grow?
complex inspection remains mum.

that as you wet you make your bed
speaks volumes as it were. tough to cook
in *völkisch* juice. a rather meager brew.

extoll cajole the same old hole. **the
penance spot of germany thou callest it.**
prow-shares of whetstones. the harvest big.

(4)

this time too is time and of german sweetness
and — darkest entry into the studbook: SMALL
OUR HANDFUL / WILD OUR STYLE — the capital old

guy deals mobilization. total / night: keeps rhenish
watch who even in the least of particles like how
or when relation feels of feelers to carapace /

senses the pelt's wolf-content yet wilfully leads
the howly pack. focus on HOW — since even
sloughing needs a snake — he burns page after

page of the *reich*'s literature in order to blacken
his face. (first man to have the extreme experience
"shrapnel." bearer of badge against dead earnest-

ness.) or WHEN elected honorary boy he mans
his all against it — but in vain! then follow
years of hits with ladies: rilkish he / gentle she

— **let no one begrudge** him **that**! meanwhile
briefly another war used in innermost chamber
to view the ur-meter. when or how he finally

his tasks accomplished happily even in death
consumes exalted earth: his mother there now!
covers him with sward that's dangerously green.

(5)

to kindly exert yourself on my behalf. the
time precise to the letter and all-merciful.
yet — would i like to be a comet? i think so.

i am! ON THE POINT of getting the point that
the feathered phrase of living bread has a
tail (even a ball after all in falling studies the

laws of fall) and am in plain english bent
upon: sometimes one would by rights construe
the word "pellet" as: regurgitated clumps

of food-scraps. spitballs. therein the half-
digested wings of brothers. there-above:
brooding blue the befitting sky. assumes

the air to be free of birds and then: letters
mob the scarecrow/syllables ruffle into
wings — i.e. are ON THE POINT or come to it.

for snipe does mean: "covered with blood"
and "twitching plunder." the tragedy of signs
in filigree. the analogous formation NAMELY

is likewise threatened. but — since come
the molting shall and must: so by and by
the flutter-phrase in torment foothold finds.

(6)

**it is asserted among men that inner ex-
cellence of man would be an assertion of
interest** — is samisdat if not clandestine.

"canonical it's not" can easily become canon-
ical. (artschwager's argument from private
speech: no sooner you intend than lo: it is!)

add moderately mantic. there seems to be
an understanding among poets nimbly to
describe the world "even if never catching

hold of it" — they say in frankfurt/oder. bit
farther west "slenderly flamed" is inked with
unfailing instinct. seems to mean formulation.

there's an unwritten rule: spiff up what you
pick up (or better yet: lift without fuss).
"there is a proposition that is unassailable

that we" can speak without having ever been
spoken. that listeners need something to chew —
is a valid handicap. as it's a trait of words that's

hard to overrate that they at best split hairs.
**accords with the belief that for arranging the world
spiritual human innerness could be of use.**

(7)

**but language — in thunderstorms speaketh the god.
often have i language it said** that LIGHTNING
was enough and spoke for itself. thinks and

knows: and so has got me! to boost this
true to type it orders signs to refuse
reference. how much of me will then be left?

leftover-me seems to have skulked on by its
standards twisted paths to sell it (reference)
cut-rate. like lead abed on the shelf you think:

i sense blood circulating in the pipes "at least"
till proof of contrary my own corporeality's
upheld. how nice i can at least still sit on it!

and oh that we might say once more: "this
would be a discovery as great as amplifying
animals." whatever that may mean it

markedly takes aim at: full circle closed/un-
broken: deification of the voice. and thunder
rumbles that now this illusion tumbles.

the drop in tension palpable "with hands"
that utan-dangling pretend grounding —
thus speaks an i that finds security in writ.

(8)

profession: poet in particular regard to copy-
right protecting the category man "of letters"
(title). content: formerly tutor in waltershausen.

now writer-in-residence berlin-mitte. was lucky /
bet on the ace of hearts: cognitive deals in poetry
and prose. shortly after came the crash.

had (no doubt his understanding of social
reality) "puffed up the act of love into a pseudo-
social super-event" and thus lost his status of

"freelance." found guilty of interpretation-theft
(cultivation of select leper-cadres) there followed
proceedings against booty-art (two years with /

three years without). meanwhile wage-dependent
he works in building-stones-grounds. (postscriptum /
to his mother: **i am now tempered through and**

**through and ordained as ye desired. i mean in the
main to stay my course. to go in fear of nothing
and tolerate much. o how reliable refreshing**

**sleep will do me good! i'm chambered almost
too splendidly. would fain have safe simplicity.
my business i hope shall prosper. fareyewell!)**

(9)

one more thing needs to be said. but not now
is the moment. when however blazes the air/
where the road runs straight through very even:

sweet landscape! a mark of wealth. full of
heat is wealth. beautiful gardens conserve the
season. then is there wealth in the simple sky?

some come to the aid of heaven. this sees the
poet. but that around me buzzeth the bee. thus it
goes. though in order to shed the warm shyness

there is happening to us in the liver an awk-
ward. you however also sense a different kind:
kleist's death. four long boards and two short.

and stuttgart. for good things come in threes.
then also of old discipline the traces. the
monastery was of use. the master however

in the wine town remains in high style. with
many tongues. but they preserve the sense.
often however like fire comes confusion of

tongues — awsome in anger cometh he then:
designating all in relation! thus it goes. but
that around me unceasingly buzzeth the bee.

LINGOS VI

mother tongues

DIN 2330: concepts and terminology. general principles.

berlin: bastion of the best. healthy-word-
begins-at-the-root-fans. strip it right down
to the morph. good. friday: work on vocab-
ulary. enter the body of language with love.

saturday: prepare stock of signs. inventory of
concepts. sunday: technical lexicon. borderline
terms. pseudo-nouns. evenings: exercises in con-
text-free association. explain "scarecrow". then

said goodbye.//vienna. b&b "the elect". here
I'm strictly by myself. problem of eyed/*i.
norms regarding low/no/free of iron verbal
fireworks. the style is up to snuff but still a

long way from the glossary to be compiled. half-
heartedly agree: "whatever's the most aid to
memory."//düsseldorf in autumn. the coolest
heads in language plight — puns will pep them up.

defence of listen-in-attack: voice prints. a first in
history. the rules seem watertight. but the word
works in lofty braille: the norm setters shall not
in vain have later """"perished simply by the trail.""""

muttersprache 1958/4:
backpack-reader. hare-dispatch.

when formulation reeks of the pen (e.g. "full
combat strength" for miles): what an enor-
mous waste of time. havoc bets on brevity.
army-speak will target the stem of the word.

watch out for prefixes! anti and counter may
in case of possibly arouse resistance. but we
know when to blow our horn: successful
sense-transfer by special letter-stuffed hare.

as if "the old long dead and rotten RUNER with his
rhymes had not been a FORSOOTHSAYER": sleeve
up! murmur at! babel on: the meatiest compounds.
may be cannonfodder bloodtoll commonweal.

no sooner do we have a free hand or brain than we
must be on a footing of war and hear the steel-bath's
coy complaint: here lies (plucked out) a leg an
arm/may god preserve us from more harm! so the

FORSOOTH- was a SOOTHSAYER after all since "on
his fickle YES AND NO hung"/or will hang "the german
fatherland's WEAL AND WOE." cf. *muttersprache* 1974/6:
thoughts on how to revive a language corpse.

muttersprache 1958/11:
struggling with the concept "stanza"

the jugness of the jug in our day has feet
of clay. rather than waver/vaccillate the
author looks for poise and takes his stand:
"it essences by being of a piece" —the editors.

bellying is of course out. for the above-
named author incorporates a form: a form
that deviates from the norm. later however
forcefully presumes: does cut not imply

form as well? agrees to visit factories. ask
about work procedures. the consequence
we know is painful stares as at the man in
the moon! here's wisdom from a potter's

mouth: if "i'm up for bids/an orphan kid" is
still grounds for creation and supposed to settle
"indexed pain" — in the appointed place. long
night of slaving over stanza-groan. no end to

the high tone. and undisclosed remains the word.
a struggle with. must writhe. how do you say
bursts into oaths: "to score" as "localized denial"?
More of this later — in the established spot.

muttersprache 1963/4:
false hare (dispatch II)

field experiment. irradiate the retina with grass.
in classic motion until quickened suddenly
appear as we had hoped the two long ears: an
analytic scalpel in these pretty rodent-poor parts.

use it in self-experiment. irradiate the retina
with quine/a strong expressive word like "weak"
— labeling can be such fun! no sooner than worst
case sets in. belabor and behoove: "mine's the

perception that/to be means to become a name"
shows nought and nothing but the use of quotes.
no charm! no "vague" that paraphrases with
precision — nought but discretion of the bard:

here I am working on a structure/that only
i can see! musters a model of immunity
but only silence on the model itself. cluster.
irradiate the retina with "........." — or

an age-old trick "this too": of hairy names
the fleece. but not a one in sight till utterly
spelled out: about my harey vision deploying
weapons of the abc— a gun's final report.

muttersprache 1968 / 1:
friend-foe-recognition

after years of toughest tinkering something like a
fresh breeze in the previous poem — rather luke-
warm though. meanwhile others are in the know.
rumor has it the dyed-in-the-wool (premature

primevals among them) are sometimes the best
workers — though prone to take face value for
achievement. so nothing much is changed for now /
the endgame relatively stable: heavyweight aesthete

vs. easy-care sports — they want to write the way
they are! HE may — not they!— and does make use
of it. first opens a paren (content no matter. here's
part for the whole his choice: where "factual fetish"

is a fitting image "image fetish" hits the factual spot.
admits a bit crazed: it could be otherwise. nevertheless
closes by itself) after the this time momentous clash:
lumpen elite vs. strengthened hermeneutic proles. at

press time the result's not in. slight suspicion quickly
proves correct: projectile is approaching target. would
mean we hope for post-strike art. in vain! the last word
is *"discorporate"* (... it urges us to leave our body).

muttersprache 1968/2:
funeral association ernst mach

if sense (true to the bylaws: spare me the experience)
accounted for the mismatch skin to market — switched
trades to say the axe in the ropemaker's house
saves what? "you've raised your arm, now whack!"

too late: he braids no more — strung up he is.
and lost to the world. is "roping in" then what
description can achieve? the answer: "spawn lives
in the smallest pond" just shows what you can do

with stumps. a leibniz reference of course. today
we'd say: how do we get the newt out the drain?
while saving the sink with economic caulk/much
ink with economic verse MAY BE a scholar's chief

endeavor the cretan paradox "world-laden"
resolved in favor of "word-soaked." in nought we
trust: if words at best in a suffix feel what they
themselves embody the reference must be a

taking. come ON you signs, take heart: you've tied
the cord, now navel! there's always pulling your-
self up — said unlicked cub re "here's the rub" —
by foreign bootstrap from now unspared sump.

muttersprache 1972 / 2:
material resistance

words don't drop out of the sky. from history they
grow. which takes forever. until (under age but
self-enslaved) animals beside their ankles sprout
antlers — magic moment: the wolf comes running

just when one cries wolf — leave it to an englishman
to "give scholasticism's speculative system the coup
de grace": let nothing stand for nothing else! the
market promptly reacts with poetry cutbacks. but

since brains (reserves "in") then are valued almost
more than bond paper (thoughts "on") there's
much to be said for not just: supply-side. almost
certainly artifice but a nose for what will work.

likewise a memorable non-word has long been
circulating round the rivers neckar ruwer spree:
a joining against the grain as that of egret and roe/
in plain speech: state-supported *verstromung*-prose.

begins the great poet famine. easy for words to
howl with the wolves. hysterically they start to
dart. power relation unclear. their sharp-toothed
jaw: producer-friendly! likely ready to tear you apart.

muttersprache 1972/4:
YO HERMENEUTICS! susan sontag declares war

to widow what's what with/cut: unramify the riddles
— a dirty business. needs to be distrusted with basedow
eyes: in complex exegetic nexus "the black stuff is
the veins." disconsolate prognosis: glandular history

droste-syndrome. essentially though ockham's meat-
braiser "you can't step twice in the same pants" that
so far lacks definitive form. fourfold interpretation
rules *okay* — even if it stops at nothing (like dead

bodies)? *YEAH!* as long as under twenty lines. remains
of text covered with cloth/star-spangled over de-
composing freight. rhymes with: how to still get
ahead be hip — through unintended guardianship.

assumed instead. but shhh! the ward's already in her
bed and dreams that "while asleep she has more weight"
at which (communal action/commondeal) the "inter-
family dirty linen gets completely out of hand:" it rages

in the basket! with a veneer of "asked for it" attempted
robbery that won't need interpretation to (de)compose
the estate. osmotic not genetic. dead fat/of human
kindness. the milk that threatens in the bodybags.

muttersprache 1978 / 1:
condition-specific art

onset of attack / scream. and autenrieth's spread arms:
"you're in good odor? you do sometimes then —
when? imagine something?" yet unkneaded the dough
keeps mum. bread too needs to be conquered. routine

treatment for now. experiments none. room with
surveillance. pain crucible — where (not for weak
nerves) he is "electroshocked until effekt." speech-
pills follow. molt ease. and doused with purest water.

who knows what he feels when in rapture / he twists
language through an early torque. manic creation.
phrases of terror we must never forget: "tomorrow,
brothers, the serviced child climbs down the hill" or

— a step in direction testines in very particular x-ray
slang: "nice shoulder this knee." knowing fingers
on high definition. ways of getting even. cold turkey.
except the chips grow back. "and what comes next"

asks navratil fragile in proxy hagen reck: "märklin-
izing pianizing maybe sometime stenographizing.
don't rightly know yet which. and well in any case
somehow go on. märklin ... and ... and ... chopin ..."

LINGOS VII

we observe the unfresh

(1)

next to nickel bloom klemm's younger granite
its mighty sudeten phase stretching from
schweinheim root horizon the organic world
thus half-witnesses emplacement of altogether

redbed flaser structure and penetrates the
latter erratically grapey-kidneyform graywacke
the dip of cauline offshoot excess aluminum
oxyde and gabbro rock says niggli stand

more or less perpendicular to dorfprozelten
outcrops of rhenish waste clay strike horn-
blende overstrikes the gneiss duct NNW
saar-selke-trough pinches the hermesbuckel

from the SE therefore doubly dessicated at the
edges bishopric bitumen hesitantly prevails
the proof: the clay as hybrid is silicified
with neutral-dappled intrudifications

(2)

continental at least in access (autobahn!)and
thus in time warp (1934-36) the oos-saale-
basin's peneplain in heidelberg-hinterland
supposedly strata of marl formations with

schlieren of marauding gangs of clay bohemian
mass the depth of fossil shells above the truly
fused layers under dross mineralized furrows
the kinds of contact zone even supercritical

plutonic rock the shut down wilhelmine-mine
final attempt on the first tubular cobalt ridge
even today there's still a stamp mill right
behind the limekiln banded deflectively in the

sense of tilt shimmering with mica where by
the aschaff river a yellow cross warns of
ymos-headquarters at the outskirts in direction
facies of certain crystalline base newts

(3)

we observe the unfresh finest rubble
ledgy-shelfy or flatly slopey under
swage space clearly geared to scale-
diameter 1 to 0.2 with waterfittings

adjusted in flat shafts sometimes late
to heal is here in handiwork so delicately
welted never waled but rather scaled as
sheared close by the road to mensengesäß

with stiff filled-in gusset by the meter
area while siskin-yellow's scarcer and
replaced by multi-lengthy due to the same
cosmic event with tendency toward as we

know frittered sinter (1722 unrecognizably
shattered) with sloping lenses hence we
advise to take a hammer the re(ad)sidual
rocks would need to be discussed by no means

(4)

nice view of wenighösbach and sprinkled
reaction-interface a mineral rest hard
hard to digest so very woolsackly in
form or implanished in mackles though

with marks of extrusion and its strain
via the knacker to the "alpine dairy"
kiosk by karlsbad law is often twinned
(let twin seams gleam) in alternate

deposits near the transformer plant by
the druid rock reception adam höllein
firm in aschaffenburg the quarrier
tanner's house near the quarry and less

striking a wayside shrine turned to rubble
clay-stone (max. 275) packed matted heap
klemm's older granite and tunnel mouths
but most of all that little transformer plant

short muddle. pores like a sieve

(1)

supposedly *MÜÜÜÜÜÜÜDE NOW* of may well be his
darling's sputum/spell listen to still wounds split open:
does she sew up his pockets alive-oh? and say that is
better? well yes she does that on the side. full time

however spreading glans of rad-unprudish kind
(dublin persuasion). unirish activities. expanded
shamrock-concept: the arctic flowers (they could
exist!) the banners of meat — good english. then

thought going ROUND the bend of the grinder would
pin down her sex — and feels: here gentle sausaging
takes place. so on according to your tongue (the urtext
anglo-swabian) the swell of *STÜRMERS*/beer mug *RITTER*

on whole or half a liter. aaah! suck is not suck as
one gets old. habeas corpus until anthrax: sore
sore! the vile old dotards bounder off. he washes
down a clot of anger. lets out a titter of despite.

(2)

then for miles just poppies. the color red remembered.
nice if pressure could be trussed. and how! after a
little dissipation the visions vanish. boldly pommel
your own quotum: expanded sweaty-concept. (hard

to decipher in the following. supposedly "formerly
lethe." then: angst out-franzed abuts estranged / where
lately we grows now past tense.) wipe clean the slate
close eyes and sponge — for christ's sake — down.

thanks! they'll soon read mysteries into this. may
we ask how: nerves too have memory? the mouth
when it chews the cud? she sews up his lips with
open-oh and says that's better. that to her mind

it's safer. seems he for countermove inclined
to let his trousers down. thus "without home" in
quasi cozy comfort shown. and does not hide that
sense grows pale. and faintly peters out the pome.

caulking

(1)

raw racketeering in the color city.
collier than hanging down the shaft.
the trawler comes with buckshot. good
luck the mobster's taking place. indoors

the alien navel corn and forfeits. it's said
they say the more the rockbed is in labor
the firedamper the schlageter. sodium and
aniline: where my cradle burst in flame.

barren ground equals being. no rock has
too much play. hungar hangar you must
hunger a wanderer between two mines. a
magyar spanner in the smelting works. self-

portrait as a young swineboy. his godfather
once went down the mine: rodenstock's speck-
schweiz. the black stuff is called coke. milling
machine. vague interest in becoming czech.

(2)

great morse-approach among the also ran-
dom recall-stumps: immediately lofoten.
scarlet unless otherwise. soon spa and
kara aka k.u.k. wanken koram van.

fatal smutty joke delighted miners shang-
haied his anheim-highness: dash-dash
man — two three-part signals! a different
matter is net weight. blood pudding

too. dot/short is in. but sermon mores
are without. a buy by light will keep
alright. the gloss will last. but now more
rent. day spent. when in the docket

the plumber flips round his own socket:
wired. let's go but keep etherialing dot
after dot through chaser oils. "the dash
I made in play..." — stop.

(3)

ahoy high-caliber patronage à la proportion-
group in tangier-urbi we're wedged down
as a jam stick to the tufa stratum of a
set-up that even among pre's will shy

away from fixes. we two construed
as occult-gnu as the test color changes
to mediate warm or umpteen-pressed
as dripping with examples lost. a

hurrah-pancake-walk through all the
agencies laps our poor pedals over the
extended grudge-goal toward an alias
gonal din-a-foundling. c/o hulling

omaha-yea-gallop-principal are we of
death his sting when that's in turn a plug-
projectile to high heaven slouches too
awed to gnaw. the piston's all that's left.

LINGOS VIII

the following

like much else is based on mishearing. informed by its
development accordingly mixes forfeited substance with
formal thanks: its status. seems faulty and like many a
thing hides nothing less than a secretion. but memory

can draw or withdraw lists. their enzyme. this for a start.
now then first resolution after er: got rand and stwhile
rant. is ectile os ubescent satz go ring mine ode. the
mouth seeks words to trigger writ. form-smith confirmed

connecting link to "creeper." (— what was the nature of
this memory? flat! how then was it compressed? deeper
yet burrows wick into flank/sniffs prick the wound etc.):
severe repulsion. then second resolution so-called high

after re: bate bellion to fine ference counting lapse.
member. and pair the parable with very verse. (past
peal fresh veal. ergo unintentionally gnomic.) verily
a huge achievement though gaping with obscene gaps.

useful or not: the wench is quenched. the rest is
handpulled proofs to correct: a vanitable pastime.
how THEN was it done. moonlighting. the third
resolution is thank god called off. but "unkind as she

is" takes a seat. gent tails and tires. collects public
pulsion lapsed late. here quest for sin presents its
pose. medial volution verbing fuse. ("...and that is
integration?" "— the only one I've heard of!")

into one mouth and out the
other: tongues. with examples.

with scissors cut paper. paper wraps stone. stone blunts scissors.
furred tongue spoke of flesh in packs on the floor cowering?
am I allowed to segregate a little piece of you? how does
right of the isar feel? and: is this a way to kiss the daughter?

with she had come out of the song-movement and she was good.
for a woman to rise to engineer with siemens. just imagine.
but always was alone. then in old age she memorized a man.
wood warbler. bismarck colony. heart infarct. (last photo: "ge-

ranium-hard his folded hands/his mouth mild": mark branden-
burg type.) with due respect for certain coded suicide orders! hence
also on: my finlandization in sommer '72 when i could suddenly
classify animal blood and how i lost this ability shortly thereafter.

with the deceased everything seems blunt: stone. scissors. even paper.
it's hard for him to tell prague from berlin. "they are so alike with
all those towers positively blunt." the departed by and by grows
stiff. "it was so long before. i once knew how. i know no more."

with for heavens' sake: are tongues here present? am I entitled to cut
a disk? so voices me let have the cheek for undeeds inconsequential?
in the original sound: flush beats straight. straight bluffs not. not
is flushed betimes. betimes it's night. and so it later came to pass

with 120 mph mouth-to-mouth: he still breathes! TONGUE-CEMENT
was used. solvent's lacking. souls automatically begin to wander.
(to paraphrase: it's easy to breathe our last and rarely rarely we
wheeze back.) armed with this certainty some then tie up the jaw.

in a state of continuing deformation

to eat something in order to which of these languages would
you like to speak — fullmouthed sounds from the lichen the
throat lab: my furry palate/the top-of-your-voice/his glottal-
stopped "we" (we four in chorus: lo ursound is present) if here

you craved conditions notarized there plaguey warriors would
have sprung up from the ground. if by the way i had the choice
i'd always take on or what gives in like brain to chemo-cudgel/
would be a fabulous hit with the shock-therapists. lippy to lock-

jaw "fauna you dog" and (beast in the sense of: nimrod's nimble
prey): who's stuck in mash shouldn't flaunt his gills or jaunt
suggestively to stonehenge for inserts ripe to be pronounced
(brief word on structure: poor disabled us the devoured threaten

to scour our guts the crows counsel to mow angry tongues
the toughs scoff: plait tender braids around the wheel (but:
which of these posited worlds would they dine on if big un-
bang: if mushroom treaty's cancelled?)) next door up against

the wall i haul back to give up/give in to incline/decline to in-
crease/begin to cry out: JUST A BRIEF WORD ON STRUCTURE my
longing/your tonguing/his stringing sometimes takes the shape
of a stingray: instray dire second sights/third would clear the

way/four out of five might in a cuntflict vote for fissured (but
only every sixth considers the excavation blood/believes in a life
in peat or bog). i'd by the way been bled (sore as before) and in
this irksome fix neither could nor was called to feel: but would!

hallelujah the lyric

look here rearing up in practically progenitive
motion one thinks perhaps of a horse and soon
in fact a stallion with his counterpart in compro-
mising would mean misjudging the situation

so creaturely so marten gnaws mouse then
"falls on gazelle" then "no better landscape for
debauch" and so on help him mount the mare
consort with animals gruesome enumeration

of what's cut off and out two broken thumbs
(the pianist) and butcher apron woe is us in
the lead bold self-mutilation here mainly
emasculate-circumstance: wire snare pruning

knife diverse axes (mostly blunt) and: who
thinks of entrails will soon read entrails he
knows they spill no longer quite fresh sur-
rounded often by carrion fans but he knows

to appreciate the pulsing the pumping longs
so much to be eaten to finally be part of being
slime one hears is something quite fine or a
rotting apple real blood to be able to say: look

i am real blood it flows but barely it doesn't
pulse or pump and has as is known "no
scythe" but thinking words but always
thinking words like technical term or tube

sting and cue

more matter! with less art! if possible however
also: more blood in mind than mind on blood —
as well as contrary of also: barely STILL! precisely
at this point the poison penetrates the sleeper's

ear: ay! leperous distilment! doth curd like eager
droppings into milk the red. an instant messenger
with letters. and barks with loathsome crust the
smooth body. this costs him a groan. and shortly —

like the kind life-rendering pelican — decamps
in limelight. only soon to transform: a handsaw
into hawk — may it betwitter him. purely a
matter of content of course. purely artificial the

attempt to train the bird his own ologist to be.
perforce crashes. at best comes to lie: in the lewd
sweat of the slithery pond where copulate the
carps of truth. devoid of howevers aside: these

are wild whirling words, my lord! we must
speak by the compass. instead of calculating
sighs it's meet the syllables to count. where
did I leave off? at "sable silvered?" "arm'd

say you"? in order by encompassment and drift
of clever question to draw near the "altogether."
less than! nevermore contra sometimes
turn to fact — see "marlowe 1593 in deptford..."

tendencies toward independence

(1)

they let it hang out as sine qua non that
if they bent their knee it certainly was
not for prayer (old school) for them the
decoy suddenly made sense — but now

they molder on in peace apparently their
relationship to corpus / totally oral to
authoritatively larynx — i mean to say
had greedy mouths to stuff at home:

these their begetters' pride in turn remained
clean sucklers and — no matter if final or ex-
pedient as long as rorschach counts — these
bellies too with spike up front soon took

their stand on the floor: trembling — may
one? may one for once say something here?
were caught trying to mimic certain injuries
that actually were caused by poisons (here

enumerate the poisons) then one morning when
the wait for monthly bleeding seemed already
vain they unexpectedly laid hand so rosy-
fingered on a space that can be taken as their

early history: for room and board had crawled
in loathsome footsteps and therefore knew
just how a sponge feels on the shovel they in
our estimate were udder and ruffian in one /

(2)

though in their own eyes thought they had
so often licked the rules (see boarding school)
that with such frequency the mere thought of
"even just once" became irrelevant. instead

craved sentence structure: which is said
to have immense effect they wanted to
preserve and were of course (consider the
asparagus) the less afraid of color change

in tests the less septic the art the more it's
a matter of certain forms of wavering (a
kind of traffic lore) so on these badmouthed
guys the ones with psalms descend like a

cord of wood: shall we? we shall! above
all keeping an eye on the ending of wasps
(countdown quidquid to agunt) and paying
by mouth the open debt was not their thing

who thought of wet in therms of "bathroom"
by no means their own — with a shudder:
to be themselves part of the steady pouring
and roaring in the pipes worth bending

your knee for (tongue in ear / ear against
wall): you hear compressed the growth of
alien cultures young green begins in
corners where lips already run riot but how

the secret life of texts

(1)

a) ... yet again and again succeeded in
standing out very agreeably. unforgotten
his portrayal of setting a dislocated
shoulder when with his hat convincingly

representing the socket he used his
free other hand to intimate both the
dislocated joint and almost playfully
the way into the yawning black...

b) "... and yet this knowledge that i call
'mine' and 'abnormal' to my knowledge
had its price which i by no means am
afraid to name 'three packs of kent' nor

do i wish to deny having settled same —
that is: in stuttered instalments and so
have done this then — or discharged
(that is: concluded the business) in order

now that i'm three good packs poorer
of the afore-invoked brand kent to use
to my own practical advantage the full
content of what's chalked up on the tick"

c) a different version plausibly asserts
the following: whoever dies this young
— and he died young — had likely more
to offer than tobacco flesh and blood

(2)

d) he hammer his tusks into the wood
where they'd been resting nesting they
equate gravity with the clutch of vise-like
claws mocking the height of the fall

swing their wings into the bluest of all
possible skies crash to make a splash
pinion first up through the clouds — where
they just were now gapes a hole

e) ...landed in a heap by the abyss the
man who indulged in tempting the gods
or: on the shoulders of the always denied
he does his hybris-thing on high

the poet: accidented but barely dented
hopes for abrasions that will remain
or rather: is and strives to be alive
though rather pressed by nature...

f) colorless but anyway it is not sudden if
what appears as image and may (or might)
be such it still proves albeit inconclusively
the sentence of the fraction we can say:

g) the
possibility
of
crows

LINGOS IX

assessing a toppled rune

all too violent the basic futhork "out of the stream
of terror swam into the swarm of enemies scream-
ing" the lines curve round now that now "this
man here assailed by a sea of corpses" a graven

"rubbed with him the tholes in the bored-out
boat" then a strong quasi-cuneiform stroke "the
worship warden am" erecting an "envy-pole"
as part of a sword belt pleases with the triple

"thistle mistle whist" animal style the double turn
of the plow "linen and leek" layed on thick as if
only one band of the sound spectrum of "same"
"not unrenowned" word-divider inroad-maker

goal-outrider this then seems what the inscription
(vistula-gothic) "spindle whorl" is about "movable
wares" successful in the quest for single rune staff
and this fart-of-a-bitch reproduction hits home

omen text "german angst"

sweat-squad at work. commando hot autumn. they
stew. hatch something. in the may of their brow. a
fearful look. the blood-axe speaks: "i'd wanted to
become an ornithologist. they have sharp ears."

now then with poetry's unwavering art of words to
bring about coherence. and lyrical blue funk. direction
kenning kaddish: too long gnawed / awed choked
on tough bone image. yet guaranteed (method

mankind) no one should wander through this world
and not harbor in his heart a hare. dispatch three.
secret fertility center — language: they SHOOT hares
don't they? what little one could comprehend — the

dead-tract-version: swabia quells four honeycomb cells.
the current they smell. a very special sap. jell-like from
the outlet spills. ultrashort hum in the room / thump
in the hive. then littleblood. smoke. symbolic swab.

loerke's moral hedgehog

antennae chloride diesel motors. while there's
general consensus that one lives in berlin one's long
been sitting in erfurt-city! with a hare's dart: con-
necting train to basel. rain. steam. accelerating speed.

misgivings: shortly after heslach they catch up: that
here cold plans are being calibrated for kidding
drunk with artifice instead of FACING the urgent
(only a matter of months) question of the seasons

— and the larch trees briskly autumn out. word-
sausage full to burst: one object every line. appears
therefore not by chance: the knouto-germanic empyre.
his versification — listen for yourself: a poem even

without zeugma nevertheless possesses muscle play —
the human tear as well as THE animal cry: i'm already
here! he by the way in those dark times came to the
sentence: proven breach of promise must be punished.

wilhelm lehmann's clinched structures

that art is surface. entrails outside the skin most
unattractive. could we then from the wound
infer the scar? here hegel ponders quite in vain:
the wound lies open to all! unproud flesh heal-

ing on either side. the more eloquently to his
taste. gathers the various. then sink into floating
uncertainty. particles like "buoys." but one's
choice may prove insufficiently sustaining.

therefore thereafter picks the gassy kinds of
words: the abstract ones. in order ("i fear this
man loves nature") to describe with twenty
different terms how the horns of oxen grow.

insists moreover craftily on wide-meshed layer-
ing: a patent trick — the bane of poetry! but
here at least beckons net gain of land: structures
of this kind need to be walked with feet!

dust culture

saussure meets sesame street. hacken-
sack. grew up there and in certain places.
where the task was. drawing information
charts. 603rd bataillon. refinement of

camouflage technique. live ammo —
ha ha ha! takes two to integrate. duck
and cover. last week's tribute: I saw
the figure five in snow. entered it

under "torso count." soldier in short
pants. maybe he got sick. could never
not forget euphorbias. let no one
listen in: then why not sneeze?

the little rock incident. arkansas. so many
love hours. moonlighting. kulchur
meets use-free beauty. died much too
young a well-paid baseball-player's son.

the man from hameln

who knows no lyrical dead wood — there can be
only one! true he was born in quedlinburg but
nevertheless marked with an aura. hardly ever
spoke himself. he let the language speak. unfailingly

on guard his ear. the oaks waft whisperings — sound
off: "finite spirits who take an interest in the physical
world are likely themselves to have bodies." the
crux of the matter: he likes to hear the song in

things. and no one could skate like him. of skating
the prodigious pleasure. formed himself through.
gave delius' sister a dressing down almost with the
left hand — let him be thanked. soon the soul's

bridegroom took up lodgings. inside him! this could
pinch. made him fall back on certain favorite old saws
— let him be forgiven. his eyes turned to the worm.
and — "now it is finished": the little worm took notice.

brockes' doctrine

of the physical poem. earthly insistence on the word.
exact examining of these to our delight lively sen-
tences. the first already lilts/lurks: a life here runs its
course. in top form bodily. which he'd been granted:

"the innumerable host/of altogether blood-filled
vessels — invisible almost" as well as "the lungs'
lubricous flesh/the stomach's acid potency/the
liver's fine capacity" to filter. him in any case out.

gradually got bloated rather. in the grand scrutinizing
face — worried at first/then suddenly serene: that
"with the lynx's pelt was carried on great commerce"
— the like of it alas is expeditious. hardly according

to his wishes. who still is rated minor-poet. best of
all possible! appreciably uneasy with his own tone.
doubts of the beetle-world. the orphaned rhymes.
the cooing gurre-lieder. disjecta membra of a poet.

amenification

this harmony. this all-coming-together. then
smack among such concepts: SAWING. surprise:
supposedly a sign of structural tyranny. supposed
thereby to disconcert. but this requires ABNORMAL

MEANS. *entartet* is explicitly not mentioned. so
the new theory has cause instead to speak of
SCRAPING. the only way for slipment to disband.
shrinkment to blossom to full height. the magic

word is "paratactic bubbling." stubbling. surely
also stumbling: the critic is on surer ground with
goethe than with eliot. discomposure of the finest.
a guest appearance. to the lectern donald davie:

"one is almost tempted to say that the rejection
of syntax in verse threatens the rule of law and
order in civilized society." yes yes: wouldn't
we like this. with minimal reservation: only!

two sentence blocks for gottlob frege

russell: as i think about acts of integrity and
grace i realise that there is nothing in my
experience to compare with frege's dedication
to truth. (...) on finding that his fundamental

assumption was in error he responded with
intellectual pleasure clearly submerging any
feelings of personal disappointment. this seemed
almost superhuman and remarkable evidence

of what men are capable of when creative work
and knowledge are at stake. wittgenstein: after
my last meeting with frege we were at the
station waiting for my train. I said to him: do

you really never see the slightest difficulty
with your theory that numbers are objects? he
replied: sometimes i almost feel as if i saw a
difficulty but then i do not see it after all.

AUTHOR'S NOTES

You may hear unidentified voices at various moments.
This is a mistake — please take no notice of them.
—Skeleton Crew

Many of the poems have quotations worked into them, which are not always marked as such. Often I could not remember where they came from, or at least can't today. For honesty's sake I want at least to mention the cases where the texts take over foreign material beyond actual quotation:

In poem II/6, "all ears especially as they of course," the poet Otto Nebel speaks several times, particularly in the case of the *versuchten einschleichtrugs* ["attempted infiltration-fraud"].

The italic passages of section III are quotes from earlier poems of mine that now feel rather foreign to me.

All boldface passages in section V are Hölderlin.

The "mother tongues" of section VI owe their title to the linguistic journal *muttersprache.* Only one title, "struggling with the concept 'stanza,'" is found as such in the journal. But there are subtle relations between the poems and the articles in the named issues.

wir beobachten unfrisches ["we observe the unfresh"] in section VII uses the vocabulary of a geological guide to the Spessart mountains: S. Matthes & M. Okrusch, *Spessart* (Berlin-Nikolassee, 1965).
kurzes geschlinge. poren wie ein sieb ["short muddle. pores like a sieve"] was written for Urs Engeler's anthology, *Erinnere einen vergessenen Text* [remember a forgotten text] (Basel, 1997) and is based on two poems by Samuel Beckett: "Enueg" and "Sanies."

stachel und stichwort ["sting and cue"] in section VIII was commissioned for the program of a Hamlet performance in Berlin-Prenzlauer Berg, which however never saw print. The material comes from Erich Fried's Shakespeare translation.

zwei satzstöcke für gottlob frege ["two sentence blocks for gottlob frege"], as indicated in the poem, is pure Bertrand Russell and Ludwig Wittgenstein. Not a word of my own.

TRANSLATOR'S NOTES

LINGOS I

p. 14. Quirinus Kuhlmann (1651 Breslau-1689 Moscow): Baroque poet and mystic whose wanderings took him as far as Istanbul, where he hoped to convert the Sultan. During his second stay in Moscow he was arrested as a heretic and sentenced to death by burning.

Jakob Michael Reinhold Lenz (1751 Livonia-1792 Moscow): Sturm-und-Drang playwright. In 1777 he suffered a nervous breakdown, which is the subject of Georg Büchner's novella *Lenz* (which ends with the words: "so he lived on"). He was found dead in a street in Moscow, presumably murdered.

LINGOS II

p. 23. "goramen": made-up word in Hugo Ball's Dada poem "caravan."

p. 24. Johann Gottfried von Herder (1744-1803): German poet, theologian and philosopher. He proposed what is now called the Sapir-Whorf thesis, that language determines thought. He also collected folk songs (*Stimmen der Völker in ihren Liedern*) and stressed the role of language and folk traditions in creating a nation.

Job: Old Testament patriarch who undergoes afflictions with fortitude and faith. Sirach: The aprocryphal book *Ecclesiasticus* is attributed to Jesus the son of Sirach.

p. 28. The poet, painter and actor Otto Nebel (1892-1973), who is quoted in this poem, was part of Dada and the Expressionist circle around the journal *Sturm*. His books *Zuginsfeld* (1918) and *Unfeig* (1923) show him to be a precursor of Concrete and combinatorial poetry. After 1933 he lived in Switzerland.

p. 31. Jakob Böhme (1575-1624): German shoemaker and mystic.

"Waspwaisted...": description of an airplane in Faulkner's *Pylon.*

LINGOS III

p. 35 Friedrich Gottlieb Klopstock (1724-1803): German poet, most famous for his epic poem, *The Messiah.* cf. p. 112 "the man from hameln."

Prater: public park in Vienna, including an amusement park with the famous Ferris wheel.

p. 36. *nichtungsdichtung:* a coinage that punningly identifies *dichtung* [poetry, literally condensation] with *nichtung,* a Heideggerian-sounding process of turning something into nothing [*nichts*].

"the knave of pain steals off": from Dylan Thomas's poem "Grief Thief of Time."

p. 37. Silesia had in the course of history belonged to Poland, Austria, Prussia. When independent Poland came into existence in 1918, the large Polish speaking population of Silesia wanted to belong to it. After three uprisings and a plebiscite, the region was divided between Poland and Germany. After WWII, most of Silesia became part of Poland.

Solingen: German city known for the manufacture of knives .

p. 39. Borussia: Old name of Prussia. Now a name for soccer teams, e.g. "Borussia Dortmund."

p. 40. "tin never IS narrow and thick": Getrude Stein, "Roast Beef."

p. 43. Gottlob Frege (1848-1925): one of the founders of modern symbolic logic.

LINGOS IV

p. 49. Joachim Schulte is an important translator and commentator of English analytical philosophy. Two of his books on Wittgenstein have been translated into English: *Wittgenstein: An Introduction* (SUNY, 1992) and *Experience and Expression: Wittgenstein's Philosophy of Psychology* (Oxford, 1995).

p. 50. "vechtation": Vechta is the birthplace of Rolf Dieter Brinkmann, whose work is to some extent a German parallel to Beat poetry.

TAUF TAUF [baptize baptize]: what St. Patrick is said to have cried when trying to christianize Ireland.

p. 51. Sils: Sils-Maria, village in the Engadine valley in Switzerland where Nietzsche and Rilke stayed.

Orplid: island paradise invented by the poet Eduard Mörike (1804-75).

Hans Vaihinger (1852-1933): German philosopher, best known for his *Philosophy of As If* (1911).

Wilhelm Waiblinger (1804-30): German Romantic poet and friend of Friedrich Hölderlin.

Johann Wilhelm Ludwig Gleim (1719-1803): German poet who is usually —wrongly—treated with condescension. Cf. the quote "soberly put..." from Jürgen Stenzel's introduction to the *Selected Poems* (Reclam).

p. 53. Ernst Herbeck (1920-91) had already spent 15 years in the psychiatric hospital of Gugging (Austria) when he began writing poems at the prompting of his psychiatrist, Leo Navratil. In 1966, a selection of his poems was published as *Alexanders poetische Texte*.

"once i too was in this kim" is a quotation from Herbeck. *kim* seems to be a neologism. It suggests *Kimme*, the rearsight notch of a gun, and the expression *jemand auf die Kimme nehmen*, to point a gun at somebody.

p. 54. Giovanni Battista Vico (1668-1744): Nepolitan philosopher and historian.

p. 55. Jena: In 1794/95 Hölderlin visited Fichte in Jena and even registered at the university.

pallaksch: a word Hölderlin made up, possibly meaning gap. In his last years, *pallaksch pallaksch* was often all he would say to a visitor. Paul Celan ends his poem on Hölderlin, "Tübingen, Jänner," with it.

LINGOS V

p. 59. "9th of march 1940" is how Hölderlin (1770-1843) dated one of his late poems ("Der Sommer").

Konradin: Duke of Svabia (1252-68). The Pope denied his election to King of Germany and his claim to the kingdom of Sicily. In 1268, aged 16, Konradin tried to reconquer his patrimony. His army defeated, he was taken prisoner and decapitated.

"year of kleist": the dramatist Heinrich von Kleist killed himself in 1811.

p. 61. *völkisch* originally meant national, but since the Nazis, the word has been strongly connected with their racist ideology.

Germany's penance spot: The German Emperor Heinrich had in 1077 been excommunicated by Pope Gregory VII. In order to be absolved the emperor had to stand for three days in the snow outside the Pope's castle in Canossa.

p. 62. The person referred to in this poem is the writer Ernst Jünger (1895-1998). He became famous with the account of his experiences in World War I, *In Stahlgewittern* [In steel storms], which glorified and aestheticized war. He published in right-wing journals in the 1920s, but refused to head the Nazi Writer's Union and, in 1938, was barred from publication. His most famous novel, *Auf den Marmorklippen* [On the Marble Cliffs] can be read as an anti-Nazi allegory.

SMALL OUR HANDFUL/WILD OUR STYLE: a Hitler Youth song.

"keeps rhenish watch": "Die Wacht am Rhein" is a patriotic/nationalistic song of 1840.

"badge against dead earnestness": The *Orden wider den tierischen Ernst* is a carneval prize usually given to witty politicians. Here, a pun on Jünger's first name.

p. 64. Richard Artschwager: American artist, born 1923.

p. 66. Waltershausen: Hölderlin was tutor there in 1894.

LINGOS VI

p. 71. DIN stands for *Deutsche Industrie-Norm,* a body of rules for anything from standard paper sizes (DIN A4) to, here, whether water may be labeled low in iron, no iron, or free of iron.

"eyed/*I" plays with the linguistic convention of starring an incorrect form or variant.

""""perished simply by the trail"""": the triple quotation marks indicate the author quoting Oskar Pastior quoting Gottfried Benn and Heinrich von Kleist.

p. 72. hare-dispatch: in German Baroque literature, secret messages are often transported in the belly of a dead hare.

p. 73. The author is Heidegger: *der Krug west im Geschlossenen des Gusses.*

p. 74. Quine: W. V. O. Quine, the American logician and philosopher.

p. 76. Ernst Mach (1838-1916): Austrian-Czech physicist and philosopher. The actual "Ernst Mach Association" (Neurath, Wittgenstein, Schlick, Carnap) was a precursor of the "Vienna Circle." The joke of "funeral association ernst mach" is that *ernst machen* means to get serious, to kill oneself.

"mismatch skin to market" puns on the expression *seine Haut zu Markte tragen,* to carry one's skin to market, i.e. to risk one's life.

"switched trades...": plays on the proverb, *die Axt im Haus erspart den Zimmermann,* an axe in the house saves [calling] the carpenter.

p. 77. *verstromung:* literally "turning into current." When needed, coal production is reoriented toward production of electricity.

p. 78. The poet Annette von Droste-Hülshoff (1797-1848) suffered from Basedow's disease characterized by goiter and protruding eyes.

p. 79. "condition-specific art" (*zustandsgebunde Kunst*) is the psychiatrist Leo Navratil's term for the art of schizophrenics. cf. note to p. 53.

J. H. F. Autenrieth: Hölderlin's psychiatrist in Tübingen.
Hagen Reck: a patient of Navratil's.

LINGOS VII

p. 83. Johann Gottlob Klemm and Paul Niggli: geologists.

p. 84. Ymos: chemical/pharmaceutical company.

p. 89. "color city:" Leverkusen because it is the site of the chemical company BASF (Badische Anilin-und Soda-Fabrik).

schlageter: a pun on *schlagende Wetter* (in mining: firedamp, air with dangerously high concentration of gas) and Albert Leo Schlageter (1894-1923). Schlageter was a member of a far-right paramilitary organization and since 1922 of the Nazi party. When Germany in 1923 fell behind with reparation payments, the French army occupied the Ruhr valley. During the ensuing fight Schlageter sabotaged the French army's supply lines, was courtmartialed and shot. He became a martyr for the Nazis.

Rodenstock is a brand of eyewear, Speckschweiz a hill near Bochum. Here mimicking an author-title-format in allusion to Gottfried Benn's lines: "my father once went to the theater/Wildenbruch's 'Crested Lark'" ("Teils-Teils").

p. 90. *k.u.k.*: abbreviation for Austria from the time when it was *königlich und kaiserlich*, royal and imperial.

Karawanken, Karakoram: mountains ranges in Austria and Pakistan.

In German, the Morse signals are called *lang* and *kurz* (long and short) rather than dash and dot.

p. 91. *din*: from DIN, German industrial norm, cf. note to p. 71.

LINGOS VIII

p. 95. Obviously the "resolutions" after "er" and after "re" yield a rather different vocabulary in German.

p. 101. *quidquid* to *agunt*: reference to the Latin proverb, *quidquid agis, prudenter agas et respice finem,* whatever you do, do it prudently and consider the outcome.

p. 103. "the sentence of the fraction" parodies poet Ernst Meister's title, *Sage vom Ganzen den Satz* [say the sentence of the whole].

p. 108. In 1972, four of the leaders of the West German terrorist group Red Army Faction (RAF), aka Baader-Meinhof Group, were captured and kept isolated in the "dead tract" area of prison Stammheim in Stuttgart, Swabia. Trying to secure their release, their followers kidnapped and killed several people. These efforts came to a head in fall 1977 ("the German autumn") with the kidnapping of a leading industrialist, Hanns-Martin Schleyer, and an airplane hi-jacking by Palestinian comrades. When the latter failed the prisoners allegedly committed suicide. It was widely believed they were assassinated.

p. 109. Oskar Loerke (1884-1941): German "nature poet" and "nature mystic." He was secretary of the poetry section of the Prussian Academy of the Arts, but gave up this post in 1933.

In the Grimm Brothers' tale, "The Hare and the Hedgehog," the hare makes fun of the hedgehog's crooked legs. The angry hedgehog challenges the hare to a race. The hare thinks he'll have no problem winning, but the hedgehog and his wife stand at either end of the racing furrow and whenever the hare arrives, more and more exhausted, a hedgehog cries: I'm already here.

p. 110. Wilhelm Lehmann (1882-1968): German "nature poet" and founder of a school of "nature-magic" with a determinedly anti-modern and apolitical stance. He postulated that a poet must "walk" (*ergehen*) his poems by hiking in nature.

p. 111. The poem refers to biographies and paintings of American painters like Marcel Duchamp, Mike Kelley, Ellsworth Kelly, Roy Lichtenstein, Ed Kienholz, Charles Demuth, Cy Twombly.

p. 112. The man from Hameln: the poet Klopstock, who grew up there. cf. note to p. 35.

p. 113. Barthold Hinrich Brockes (1680-1747): German Baroque poet. His main multi-volume work, *Irdisches Vergnügen in Gott* [earthly delight in god], was scorned by Schiller, but influenced poets like Herder and Mörike.

p. 114. Many quotes come from Hugo Friedrich's anti-modernist *Struktur der modernen Lyrik*.

ON AUTHOR & BOOK

Ulf Stolterfoht was born in 1963 in Stuttgart and now lives in Berlin with his wife and three children. He has published 3 books of poems, all called *Fachsprachen* [lingos, jargons, technical terms]:
Fachsprachen I-IX (1998), *Fachsprachen X-XVIII* (2002), which received the Hans Erich Nossack-Förderpreis and the Christine Lavant-Preis respectively, and most recently, in 2004, *Fachsprachen XIX-XXVII* for which he received the Anna-Seghers-Prize in 2005 and a fellowship to the German Academy in Rome..

Lingos I-IX takes as its playground all the cultural baggage of our turn of the century and examines it with a mix of deconstruction, parody and sheer exuberance. The poems flaunt their intent to avoid linearity, reference, prefabricated meaning and, especially, the lyrical I. Instead, they cultivate irony, punning, fragmenting, juxtaposing, distorting, and subject everything to an almost compulsive humor — the author and his own methods included.

Of the main targets, literary theory, contemporary philosophy and the German poetic tradition, the latter suffers most in translation. For a German reader, *er verb es genau* [he verb it just right] invokes Goethe's "Erlkönig:" *ich weiss es genau/es scheinen die alten Weiden so grau*. Likewise *ein ganz besondrer Saft* [a very special sap] is recognized as blood because Mephistopheles calls it so in Faust — to mention just two of the many instances. This texture of allusions disappears almost completely in the English version, except for occasional quotes from Shakespeare ("sting and cue"), Beckett (the two poems of "short muddle. pores like a sieve"), and, less obviously, Gertrude Stein ("tin never IS narrow and thick"), Dylan Thomas ("the knave of pain steals off") or Faulkner's description of airplanes from *Pylon* (p. 31).

The poems are in stanzas, but their form has been fittingly described as an amalgam of quantity and rectangle. Lines with regular meter are set against deliberately prosaic ones. Rhyming words are heaped in quick succession as a send-up of poetic convention, but will also be used in a more traditional manner to tie together sequences of words. For instance in II/6 (p. 28), the Expressionist painter/poet Otto Nebel paints in obedience to inner voices that also tell him to hang himself. The homophony *horchen gehorchen* [listen obey] is crucial for the poem. But, in addition, there is the sequence *zwang — drang — befehlsergang — hanf — schlang*, where the rhyme gives extraordinary power to the connection of compulsion, urge, and eventual suicide by hanging.

The translator has done what she can and, while mourning the impossible perfect translation, hopes at least to approximate the pleasure of Stolterfoht's lingos.

SELECTED BURNING DECK BOOKS:
ONE SCORE MORE: THE SECOND 20 YEARS OF BURNING DECK, 1982-2002.
PEGASUS DESCENDING: A BOOK OF THE BEST BAD VERSE, ed. J. Camp, X. J. Kennedy & K. Waldrop.
Walter Abish: *99: THE NEW MEANING.* Collage texts.
Beth Anderson: *OVERBOARD.* Poetry.
Rae Armantrout: *PRECEDENCE.* Poetry.
Alison Bundy: *DUNCECAP.* Stories.
Robert Coover: *THE GRAND HOTELS (OF JOSEPH CORNELL).* Prose.
Susan Gevirtz: *HOURGLASS TRANSCRIPTS.* Poetry.
Peter Gizzi: *ARTIFICIAL HEART.* Poetry.
Barbara Guest: *THE COUNTESS FROM MINNEAPOLIS.* Poetry.
John Hawkes: *INNOCENCE IN EXTREMIS.* Novella.
Janet Kauffman: *FIVE ON FICTION.* Fiction / Theory.
Elizabeth MacKiernan: *ANCESTORS MAYBE.* Novel.
David Miller: *STROMATA.* Poems.
Claire Needell: *NOT A BALANCING ACT.* Poetry.
Gale Nelson: *STARE DECISIS.* Poetry.
—: *CETERIS PARIBUS.* Poetry.
Ray Ragosta: *VARIETIES OF RELIGIOUS EXPERIENCE.* Poetry.
Elizabeth Robinson: *UNDER THAT SILKY ROOF.* Poetry.
Pam Rehm: *THE GARMENT IN WHICH NO ONE HAS SLEPT.* Poetry.
Stephen Rodefer: *PASSING DURATION.* Prose poems.
W. D. Snodgrass: *SIX MINNESINGER SONGS.* Printed with the original melodies.
Marjorie Welish: *THE WINDOWS FLEW OPEN.* Poetry.
Dallas Wiebe: *SKYBLUE'S ESSAYS.* Prose.
—: *THE VOX POPULI STREET STORIES.* Novel.
Elizabeth Willis: *TURNERESQUE.* Poetry.

SERIE D'ECRITURE:
CROSSCUT UNIVERSE: Writing on Writing from France, ed./trans. Norma Cole. Texts by Albiach, Bousquet, Collobert, Daive, DuBouchet, Fourcade, Guglielmi, Hocquard, Lewinter, Ronat, Roubaud, Royet-Journoud.
Anne-Marie Albiach: *A GEOMETRY.* Trans. K. & R. Waldrop. [chapbook]
Pierre Alferi: *OXO.* Trans. Cole Swensen.
Marie Borel: *CLOSE QUOTE.* Trans. Keith Waldrop. [chapbook]
Marcel Cohen: *THE PEACOCK EMPEROR MOTH.* Stories. Trans. Cid Corman.
Jean Daive: *A LESSON IN MUSIC.* Trans. Julie Kalendek.
Suzanne Doppelt: *RING RANG WRONG.* Trans. Cole Swensen.
Jean Grosjean: *AN EARTH OF TIME.* Trans. Keith Waldrop.
Emmanuel Hocquard: *A TEST OF SOLITUDE.* Sonnets. Trans. Rosmarie Waldrop.
Paol Keineg: *BOUDICA.* Trans. Keith Waldrop.
Pascal Quignard: *ON WOODEN TABLETS: APRONENIA AVITIA.* Trans. Bruce X.
—: *SARX.* Trans. Keith Waldrop. [chapbook]
Jacqueline Risset: *THE TRANSLATION BEGINS.* Trans. Jennifer Moxley.
Claude Royet-Journoud: *i.e.* Trans. Keith Waldrop. [chapbook]
Esther Tellermann: *MENTAL GROUND.* Trans. Keith Waldrop.
Alain Veinstein: *EVEN A CHILD.* Trans. Robert Kocik & Rosmarie Waldrop.